THE AMERICAN LIBRARY

10, RUE DU GÉNÉRAL CAMOU
75007 PARIS

THE TRANSIENT GLEAM

A Bouquet of Beckford's Poesy

The Transient Gleam

THE TRANSIENT GLEAM

A Bouquet of Beckford's Poesy

Presented by

DEVENDRA P. VARMA

Foreword by

BROCARD SEWELL

First published 1991 by
The Aylesford Press

THE TRANSIENT GLEAM
Copyright © Devendra P. Varma 1991

Foreword © Brocard Sewell 1991

British Library Cataloguing in Publication Data
Beckford, William, *1760–1844*
  The transient gleam: a bouquet of Beckford's poesy.
  I. Varma, Devendra P. *1923–*
821.6

ISBN 1 86995-512-9

Printed in Great Britain
THE HILBRE PRESS
Wirral, Cheshire

Bound in Great Britain
THOMAS LOUGHLIN
Liverpool, Merseyside

ACKNOWLEDGEMENTS

ON A COLD, wind-blown winter twilight I stood with
Father Brocard Sewell in front of Beckford's grave and read
the epitaph. Under the shadow of Beckford's Tower he first
sparked my interest in Beckford's poetic genius. Thanks are
due to David Ashton of The Aylesford Press for having
suggested this anthology of Beckford's poems to coincide
with the Beckford Round Table at the Eighth International
Congress on Enlightenment, at Bristol in 1991. Didier Girard
of Paris obtained for me the copies of original epitaphs and
rendered sound advice. Lidia Kaczurowskyj of Munich
supplied difficult translation pieces; Aurelia Hepkema of
Geneva tracked some invisible Beckford trails for me in
Venice and Switzerland, while Margaret Brown of the Shelley
Museum filled some important gaps during these quests. The
special catalogue of Beckford papers compiled by T.G.
Rogers at the Bodleian was indeed helpful and information
received from Leslie and Elizabeth Hilliard of the Beckford
Tower Trust eased many arduous tasks. Jon Millington, the
scholar and collector of Beckfordiana, disentangled many
perplexing points and guided me through researches into a
vast mass of manuscripts and papers. He personally, and
through The Beckford Trust, gave great help with the
illustrations. And he kept me constantly supplied with
rarities. V.J. Kite provided me with personal support in
locating and obtaining some rare Beckford items, while
Kenneth W. Graham and Malcolm Jack gave much needed
encouragement and ideas when I seemed to run into a blank
wall. I am conscious of the guidance and generosity of James
Lees-Milne, the doyen of Beckford studies, who kindly
indicated some valuable lines of thought and development.
To A.T.M. Moriarty goes my special indebtedness and
gratitude for hospitality and assistance during research trips
in Wiltshire, and long drives together in remote corners of

8

Britain exploring musty bookshops and arranging numerous interviews with old booksellers and collectors. The pictures and engravings supplied by the courtesy of William Morris and George Bayntun of Bath are gratefully acknowledged. I am particularly indebted to Dr H.S. Whittier, my scholarly colleague, who with his penetrative insight and deeper analysis of individual poems enlightened me at every step. Thanks are due to Professor James Gray who spared neither time nor trouble in streamlining this project, and whose discussions and ungrudging advice made this venture possible.

DEVENDRA P. VARMA

CONTENTS

ILLUSTRATIONS

FOREWORD

IN 1962 BOYD ALEXANDER, custodian of the Beckford
papers at Hamilton Palace, believed that Beckford had
written only two poems, 'The Last Day' and 'A Prayer'. A
strange computation, for surely he must have known the
'incidental' poems in Beckford's *Azemia* and *Modern Novel
Writing*; but perhaps he did not take these seriously? In any
case, most of Beckford's poems had appeared anonymously,
in periodicals of the day. To identify and assemble them
would have been a difficult task; a task unattempted, as far as
I know, until now. So all who are interested in the life and
works of William Beckford must be grateful to Professor
Varma for his researches and for this delightful anthology
which is sure to ignite further explorations into Beckford's
poetry.

Swinburne, in a letter to Mallarmé written in French in
1876, says of Beckford that 'To be a millionaire and want to
be a poet and only to be half a one' must have made the life of
this poet *manqué* gloomy indeed. But we do not know
precisely what value Beckford placed on his poems. He
certainly looked on them as something more than *jeux
d'esprit*. We may perhaps think 'The Last Day' a not very
successful rendering of the opening stanzas of the '*Dies irae*',
but 'A Prayer' is emphatically a fine poem, with true religious
feeling.

Of course, not all his verse is on this level, nor was it
intended to be. The 'Ode, Panegyrical and Lyrical', from
Modern Novel Writing, attacking Beckford's *bête noire*
William Pitt, is a splendid hate poem, and the witty 'Enigma'
(from the same source) offers a challenge to the crossword-
puzzle-minded of today.

In a letter to the Chevalier Franchi, written in 1815,
Beckford says: 'The thought that the day is not distant when
all that I have done or am doing will dissolve into thin air fills

me with a bitter melancholy.' In 1825 the tower of the Abbey at Fonthill did, almost literally, dissolve into thin air; but was replaced by the more elegant tower of Lansdown. And if Beckford could have foreseen the wonderful 'William Beckford at Fonthill' pageant, attended by three thousand people, that was enacted on the greensward in front of the sole surviving portion of the Abbey on a summer afternoon in 1986, he would never have said that himself and all that he had done or tried to do was destined for oblivion. The paradise that he opened in the wild, though difficult of access today, is not obscured. Beckford remains, for all his quirks and oddities, a light that shines.

BROCARD SEWELL

Beckford's Tower, Lansdown

Fonthill Abbey

INTRODUCTION

THE TRANSIENT GLEAM

> *"Eternal Power!*
> *Grant me, through obvious clouds, one transient*
> * gleam*
> *Of thy bright essence in my dying hour!"*

EXOTIC FLOWERS still bloom and wilt in the crannies and fissures of the fallen bricks and mortar of Fonthill, wafting a strange soft incense on the evening air. As wild roses and drooping azaleas softly sway among the thorns and brambles across the green sward path, we conjure up fond memories of William Beckford, the builder of Fonthill — artist, dreamer, visionary, connoisseur of paintings and *objets d'art*, lover of books — poet and the author of *Vathek*. We envision him sauntering through leafy haunts and wilderness, lost in thought, forgetful of time and place, musing and dreaming; or riding across the bare hills gazing over far spreading landscapes at sunset.

No attempt has ever been made to collect and publish Beckford's poems from extinct journals and his prose works, nor any sustained effort directed by scholars to follow the sequence or development of their themes, thought or motivation. These may not provide any significant peep into some great philosophy or inaugurate discussions of poetic theories, but they do mirror a particular rhythm of life and a unique poetic vision.

Under the shadow of Beckford's Tower on Lansdown, the moving lines inscribed on his solid granite tomb are an admission of agnosticism with a desperate hope for some sort of salvation and immortality. He certainly achieved the latter, but did he catch the 'transient gleam' or even a faint glimmer of Celestial light?

We have been dazzled by Beckford's fantasies, his taste for the Oriental and fantastic, love of flowers and perfume, his collections of paintings, the extravagant intensity and lashings of gold, crimson and purple. His account of the strange necromantic lights of the Demon temple, visions of the lonely damned, were reminiscent of Sufi poets like Hāfiz and Firdausi, and their philosophical concepts. But we can break through the crust of his physical fancy, his knowledge of the invisible and occult speculations, when we balance these against his observation of the grim and grotesque, tender and comical aspects of mortal existence.

Beckford's imagination was *religious*, not *fantastic*. His mystic vision suggested a realm of existence hidden behind the world of reality. But he saw the sad predicament of man's fate illuminated by flashes of light, moments of joy, and dreams of romantic loveliness.

A combination of social pressures, injured spirit and the desire to contrive a sanctuary for himself turned Beckford into a recluse. This earliest of Romantics, often called England's 'Kubla Khan', who indulged in the most lavish folly of Romantic architecture where he fed on dreams of Xanadu, was naturally creative in flights of fancy and inspiration. But his poetry was better expressed perhaps in his dream-like prose, much of which reveals the trance-like, languid, aspect of his muse; his ear was so musical, so sensitive to sound and lilt — would it not have been surprising if he had *not* written verse?

We discern both power and pathos in his short pieces of poetry. And there is not the slightest doubt that Beckford composed a great deal in prose and verse, which either has been destroyed by him or still exists in manuscripts. In a letter to the Revd Thomas Maurice, he mentions 'my poetic Trifles', and adds 'Should I be hereafter induced to bring into the Light any of the contents of my portfolio whether in prose or rhyme, I shall do myself the Honour to request your Acceptance of them. . .' It is known that some of his verses were privately circulated, a fact borne out by the *European*

Magazine for September 1797: 'In prose and verse; . . . in point of genius, wit and classic composition, [he is] not second to the most distinguished.'

Indeed, there is something strange, yet fascinating, about the spirit of his pen. 'His good prose might have been admirable verse,' remarked one of his critics. In imagination and poetic power of evocation, in expression and rhythm of phrases, his exotic prose not only appeals to our eyes, but also enthralls our ears. A literary critic reviewing *Italy* in the *Athenaeum* of June 21, 1834, wrote:

> This is no more a book of travels than Childe Harold's Pilgrimage — it is a prose poem . . a record of impressions . . scenes not to be excelled in modern poetry — pictures where words are as rich in colour and in beauty as the pencil of Turner.

Beckford once confessed that if someone 'spurns the malign control of the crowd . . . his cheerfulness can subdue affliction, and he can sing like a nightingale to charm the lonely hour . . . (in) glorious songs.' Time and Change turn the past into fading 'phantoms'. Memory and Fancy embodied in poetic art can revivify these phantoms and overcome their apparent fading or subjection to the ravages of Time and Absence. This value he placed on isolation also implied his view of worldly concern and nature. He could write seriously on Death as well as pen a comic epitaph, thus revealing his strong sense of detachment and impersonality.

One cannot be oblivious to the fact that he hardly produced any cogent prose piece between 1790 and the 1830s. Writing letters, composing short poems, designing spoons, teapots or candelabras had become his major preoccupations in the secluded world of Fonthill. The Abbey had become so absorbing that Beckford did not concentrate on long and substantial prose work.

Why did Beckford write poems, and that too anonymously? Possibly he was reluctant to have his name associated with an art-form in which he felt he did not excel. His prose works were also, for the most part, published anonymously or pseudonymously, probably in an attempt to protect himself from unkindly criticism. After 1784, one suspects, he did not wish to revive the scandal awakened by the mention of his name. He recoiled from the mud of political formalities and intrigue into the glorious haven of literature and art. Once he mentioned to Cyrus Redding, his biographer: 'I am no solitary, but I would rather live in hermit solitude, than in the turmoil of faction and political intrigue.'

While steeped in Oriental studies, young Beckford practised the art of poesy. It is easy to perceive that those early metrical experiments were in the strain of Goldsmith, Cowper, Blair, Thomson, Collins, etc., youthful effusions that caught the music of purling streams and wafted the perfume of zephyrs against the scenic backdrops of shepherds and groves. These were simple and natural ruminations rather than samples of any complex, indefinite or incomprehensible poetic visions, and were mostly designed to be included in prose works. In many instances he mocked the fashionable poetic vein of his time, especially the Scottish verses, but his better productions were very often concerned with Death and Religion.

Beckford's poems fall into three distinctive groups: the early poems drenched in fanciful reveries, religious poems, and epitaphs written at Fonthill, during his twilight years. For a continuous thread, one discerns two repeated elements: an attraction to a motif of sequestration or seeking after protective enclosures, the other being a flair for satire. Beckford believed himself to be a wit; but his sense of irony is more persuasive than his capacity for satire.

The motive of Beckford's poetry stems perhaps from an urge to question the purpose and consequence of mortal existence. Yet, while the religious poems deserve serious consideration, he did not have any strong or obsessive interest in religion and its major components like *decorum* and the notion of *Fate*. But certainly 'A Prayer' and 'The Last Day' are a manifestation of his own brand of religion.

He had profound ideas about the wisdom and goodness of the Supreme Being. These he sometimes mingled with his enjoyment of picturesque nature, his love of which was intense, seeing all with a poet's eye — the wilder, the more attractive. Describing *Nature*, was for Beckford, just as for

Chateaubriand, an opportunity to blend religion and poetry in a typically aesthetic way like a landscape painting. His preference for studious pursuits never overshadowed his enjoyment of nature and art, which remained his great solace and delight.

Amongst his early experiments, 'To orisons, the midnight bell' is an astonishing maiden attempt by a teenager, depicting a striking scene and evoking a vivid recollection of a grand solitude. These solitary musings combined with a command of language foreshadow the literary qualities of his subsequent poetic endeavour. The interesting structure and perspective of this poem exalt Beckford as a spiritual link between the recluse and the external world.

Once again, 'Prayer' stresses the relationship between isolation and wisdom, and calls for 'communing with God'. Interestingly, it contains some lines apparently intended for his own epitaph. He addresses the all-pervading spirit and begs for a 'transient gleam'; he asks for just a glimpse, for the predicament of isolation from this world has shrouded that 'gleam', preventing him from receiving the blessing and radiance of God.

Sufi poets like Omar Khayyam had been mystified by the veil beyond which we cannot see; Tennyson had desired to see his 'Pilot face to face'; to Wordsworth the Celestial Light got lost after childhood, but Beckford had no reminiscence of it. Shakespeare may well have glimpsed through that veil in Hamlet's ghost. In Beckford we get the only link with 'Hope' in *Vathek*!

Another poem, 'The Last Day', sounds forth the Voice of Judgement. Beckford rises to the point that conscience is consciousness of one's actions, for our sense of guilt unfolds through our conscience. The *Bhagavadgita* had explained that karma (action) is our censure, or that conscience is the motivation of karma. These are not superficial influences; they have deep relevance in the mosaic of Beckford's ruminations.

In his rambles over the continent, he visited hermitages and monasteries nestled in the hills, and amused himself by making extracts from albums kept in those picturesque places. He formed certain impressions on the spot, and a few poems resulted from his musings. Beckford wrote 'Napoleon' in the manner of *Childe Harold*, but 'Ætna' echoes more Byronic qualities.

Beckford painted the emotion of love from various angles, 'On a Dead Goldfinch' is a pleasant comic caricature of a lover as a pet bird. In a humorous poem, 'Verses', another enjoyable piece in the nature of a joke, this serious emotion is treated flippantly. 'Ah, well-a-day!' is a specimen of a *jeu d'esprit*, a comic comment upon marriage without any edge of satire. 'When you are absent all look drear'ly' is a straight assertion on love with an alternate lapse into melancholia.

Following the prevalent poetic vein of the novelists of the 1790s 'What is this sentimental love' contrasts sentimentality and love. These pieces were written in the manner of the late 18th century verses published in old magazines in the popular Rosa Matilda style, but often exaggerated for effect of caricature. Rosa was actually Charlotte Dacre, a disciple of 'Monk' Lewis, who penned such amorous romances as *Zofloya*, *Passions*, *Libertine*, and *Confessions of the Nuns of St. Omer*.

But Beckford's touching piece 'Conjugal Love — An Elegy' asks us not to attempt any romantic height of idealised love but to exercise a more constrained view which rewards a 'mild domestic life.' To lose oneself in the happiness of others is the means to attain greatest happiness. The continuity of life streams through conjugal love: children, offspring, progeny, where the self or soul is not dead but reincarnated. The poem closes with the thought of continuity after death, in Heaven.

One cannot but admire his manifold experiments for the quality and variety in the sheaf of his assorted poems. 'A Swiss Day' bears a post-Augustan style, tone and sensibility: a celebration of the abstract view of visible nature ending with the comparison between the Calm of the evening and Death. An admirable burlesque, 'When howling winds and louring skies', is a prayer for respite from the ravages of the storm at sea. 'On the Wreck of a Brig off Dunwich' is like a ballad and has a tripping metre; it could be sung like a folk-song. The poet speaks to a listener in 'Ere yet your footsteps quit the place'. But the listener is none other than Beckford himself!

He notes that it was 'written, at the close of winter, to a friend, just leaving a favourite retirement, previous to settling abroad.' Perhaps this title was given to conceal his own self reference, for it is obvious that he is recording his own sentiments on the eve of his departure for Switzerland. The romantic South and its scenery had exerted a magnetic influence upon his mind. The poem is a celebration of nature's loveliness through three seasons — spring, summer, autumn. Remembrance and fancy turn the phantoms of the past into something constant and unfading.

Beckford's poems lie scattered in The *Literary Gazette*, *Western County Magazine*, *Gentleman's Magazine*, in poetical albums, *Mirror of Literature*, and *Talisman*, etc. The Bodleian today prizes the resurrected archive of Beckford's entombed papers, the surviving fragments of his original manuscripts, drafts of poems, collection of unpublished verses and the epitaphs.

It has been difficult to locate the source for 'The Calm' by the late William Beckford Esq., perhaps his last poem, dated 1844, which appeared posthumously. It is a Petrarchan sonnet, a subtle blend of Augustan and Romantic sensibility with pictorial effects of idealised Nature and idealised society. The octave contains a description of natural scenery observed after a storm, with pastoral views 'gilded' by the Sun where visible nature smiles under light and showers. The sestet describes the pleasures of rural life, and of men in a natural state, whom the poet calls sons of liberty.

In his rambles through some forlorn cemeteries on the high road from London to Bristol, Beckford had deciphered some 'whimsical' and 'nearly effaced' inscriptions upon dilapidated tomb-stones. Under the pseudonym of 'Viator' he addressed a letter about them to The *Literary Gazette* from Bath in October 1822. While some of these are genuine, a great number are his own compositions, often inscribed on odd scraps of paper, old letters, margins of bills, and so forth. These epitaphs, though sometimes satirically comic and burlesque in vein, often express genuine despair and sorrow. There are invectives against doctors who kill patients, and satirical thrusts at a clergyman who was not a fox-hunter but aimed at human souls! There is also reference to drunkenness and its consequences.

These indicate that Beckford displays a cheerful attitude towards death in a gently comic way. The rhythm and metrical arrangement have an incisiveness like that of Pope's couplets characterized by playful wit or satiric good humour. Such keen and polished satire is too sharp for the uninstructed in that quiet kind of censure, but contain sparks for the intelligent to comprehend.

Beckford approached *Death* in many forms and ways. His serious irony is reflected in comic form, while at other times he comments on grotesque forms of Death. 'Ye who the merits of the dead revere' is a profoundly penetrating view of Lady Barton's creative powers revealed through sensitive and pervasive irony. The satire becomes keen and polished in the juxtaposition of her talent and madness. In the rational world, creative talent is only an eccentricity or lunacy, — perhaps a self-analysis of the poet himself!

In addition to some verses from *Azemia* and *Modern Novel Writing*, it has been found expedient to include the Fonthill poems for they mirror Beckford's life-style, his archaeological interests, his eccentricities balanced against the conventional and transient nature of existence. Fonthill, the most splendid edifice ever seen or fancied, except in fairy-tales, was the creation of genius, taste and power. Though the interest of Fonthill is essentially local, the multitude of circumstances connected with the place generalises and extends its appeal. These poems carry it out of the pale of mere topographical, antiquarian, and architectural interest into the realm of popular curiosity. Art bestows an apparent immortality on the ephemeral nature of worldly fame. Art obliterates the limitations of Time. Nature consumes all human achievements, but the absolute Power of Time can be alleviated by Art alone, which can be perceived in the continuity of Life observed in Nature.

'On a First View of Fonthill Abbey' appeared in *Fonthill Abbey and Demesne* by John Rutter (Shaftesbury 1822); John Jefferson's 'Fonthill' was published in Blandford in 1824; 'Beckford's Tower' by W. Gregory Harris first appeared in the *Bath and Wilts Chronicle and Herald* in 1933; 'Fonthill Abbey' by E.K. written in 1827, was found among press cuttings tipped in the Bath Lending Library's copy of Cyrus Redding's *Memoirs of William Beckford* (1859). 'Fonthill' appeared in The *Anniversary* for 1829, edited by Allan Cunningham. In *Memoirs of William Beckford* by Cyrus Redding, there is a verse quoted entitled 'Thoughts suggested in Mr. Beckford's Park, the day after his decease', a tribute of respect full of genuine feeling:

'The master is departed from his place . . . etc.'

It was in Fonthill that Beckford stood aloft 'wrapt in his cloak of learning and of wit', with 'a mind of fire, a deeply feeling heart', and as 'a stranger to our sphere'.

A glance at the choicest books in his bounteously enriched collection hint at Beckford's taste and love for the poetic muse. Among Oriental writings he highly prized those of Hãfiz the Persian poet whose *Divan* was one of his special favourites. Beside the Greek and Latin Classics, the embossed and gilt editions of Dante, Milton, Tasso, Dryden, Pope, Gray, Thomson, Moore, Southey, Cowper, Goldsmith and several others graced his shelves. He loved the poems of Camoens and the Odes of Anacreon, and had a particular fascination for Petrarch whose following few lines he could well have composed himself:

O giorno, o ora, o ultimo momento
O stelle, congimate a' impoverirme!
O Fido, squardo a che volei tu dirme,
Partend' io, per non esser mai contento?

DEVENDRA P. VARMA
DALHOUSIE UNIVERSITY

LYRICAL POEMS

ODE

To orisons, the midnight bell
Had toll'd each silent inmate from his cell;
  The hour was come to muse, or pray,
Or work mysterious rites that shun the day:
  My steps some whisp'ring influence led,
Up to yon pine-clad mountain's gloomy head:
  Hollow and deep the gust did blow,
And torrents dash'd into the vales below:
  At length, the toilsome height attain'd,
Quick fled the moon, the sudden stillness reign'd.
  As fearful turn'd my searching eye,
Glanc'd near a shadowy form, and fleeted by;
  Anon, before me full it stood;
A saintly figure, pale, in pensive mood.
  Damp horror thrill'd me till he spoke,
And accents faint the charm-bound silence broke:
  'Long, trav'ller! ere this region near,
'Say did not whisp'rings strange arrest thine ear?
  'My summons 'twas to bid thee come,
'Where sole the friend of Nature loves to roam.
  'Ages long past, this drear abode
'To solitude, I sanctified, and God:
  ''Twas here, by love of Wisdom brought,
'Her truest lore, self-knowledge, first I sought;
  'Devoted here my worldly wealth,
'To win my chosen sons immortal health.

'Midst these dun woods and mountains steep,
'Midst the wild horrors of yon desart deep,
   'Midst yawning caverns, wat'ry dells,
'Midst long, sequester'd ailes, and peaceful cells,
   'No passions fell distract the mind,
'To Nature, Silence, and Herself consign'd.
   'In these still mansions who shall bide,
' 'Tis mine, with Heaven's appointment, to decide;
   'But, hither, I invite not all:
'Some want the will to come, and more the call;
   'But all, mark well my parting voice!
'Led, or by chance, necessity, or choice,
   '(Ah! with our Genius dread to sport)
'Sage lessons here may learn of high import.
   'Know! Silence is the nurse of Truth:
'Know! Temperance long retards the flight of Youth:
   'Learn here, how penitence and pray'r
'Man's fallen race for happier worlds prepare:
   'Learn mild demeanor, void of art,
'And bear, amidst the world, the hermit's heart.
   'Fix, trav'ller! deep this heaven-taught lore:
'Know, Bruno brings it, and returns no more.'
   (Half sighed, half smiled his long farewell.)
He turn'd, and vanish'd in the bright'ning dell.

THE LAST DAY

'Dies iræ, Dies illa!'

Hark! heard ye not that deep, appalling sound?
Tremble!—for lo the vex'd, the affrighted ground
Heaves strong in dread convulsion—streams of fire
Burst from the vengeful sky—a voice of ire
Proclaims, 'Ye guilty, wait your final doom:
No more the silent refuge of the tomb
Shall screen your crimes, your frailties. Conscience reigns,—
Earth needs no other sceptre;—what remains
Beyond her fated limits, dare not tell;—
Eternal Justice!—Judgment!—Heaven!—Hell!'

A PRAYER

Like the low murmurings of the secret stream,
    Which through dark alders winds its shaded way,
My suppliant voice is heard: ah, do not deem
    That on vain toys I throw my life away!

In the recesses of the forest vale,
    On the wild mountain, on the verdant sod,
Where the fresh breezes of the morn prevail,
    I wander lonely, communing with God.

When the faint sickness of a wounded heart
    Creeps in cold shudderings through my sinking frame,
I turn to Thee—that holy peace impart
    Which soothes the invokers of Thy august name.

O all-pervading spirit—sacred beam!
    Parent of life and light!—Eternal Power!
Grant me, through obvious clouds, one transient gleam
    Of Thy bright essence in my dying hour!

When on a clear and cloudless night
The moon shall pour her level light,
   And tremble on the silver sea;
I then shall watch her cheering rays,
And sighing ask, if thou dost gaze
   On her bright orb—and think of me?

When raving fierce through every shroud
The wild careering wind is loud,
   And I on the mid watch shall be;
My heart will ask, as tempests rise,
If thou dost hear?—and gentle sighs
   Heave thy soft heart, while pitying me?

If destin'd in the bloody fight
To close these eyes in endless night,
   That now so fondly gaze on thee;
Even then, as life shall ebb away,
My latest lingering breath shall say,
   My only love!—remember me!—

Beckford's Tomb at Bath

William Beckford

Ill-earn'd applause! how bitter is thy smart
To those who praise exclusive only love!
How light, compar'd, all other sorrows prove!
Thou shedd'st a night of woe, from whence depart
The poetesses patience; and the heart
'Mid lesser ills illume: shall Sheeppen rove,
On the high summit of Parnassian grove,
Blank *Versificator*?—Alas! thy dart
Kills more than life poetic—all that's dear,
Till we, so mortified and pain'd, would change
For phrensy that forgets malicious tear,
Or wish in non-poetic fit to range
Where moon-revolving Fashion loves to sip
Her mawkish draught, or skims with flirting trip.

SONG

Love is a soft, involuntary flame,
  Beyond the pow'r of language to express;
That throws resistless magic o'er the frame,
  And leads to boundless pleasure or distress.

From love misfortune takes her earliest date,
  Or rapt'rous bliss prepares the flow'ry way;
Wak'd at our birth, they mingle with our fate,
  And cling to life, till vanquish'd by decay.

E'en when in youth we feel the hand of death
  Obscure the prospect of a cloudless sky.
All conqu'ring love attends the fleeting breath,
  And Nature's fond, last effort, is a sigh.

Then tell me, Henry! what avail the cares
  . That taint our joys with bitterness and pain?
If to our aid the god of love repairs,
  And Henry smiles, misfortunes frown in vain.

ENIGMA

I'm as firm as a rock, and as weak as a reed,
As slow as a snail, and as swift as a steed,
As fat as a porpoise, yet thin as a rake,
As pliant as ozier, though stiff as a stake.
I'm a giant, a dwarf, a lion, a hare,
And by fetters constrain'd, am as free as the air.
Extremely deform'd, yet a beauty complete,
Very fat, very thin, and tho' dirty am neat.
I can fly like an eagle, but can't leave the ground,
Am exactly a square, and am perfectly round,
I'm as heavy as lead, and as light as a fly,
And am at a distance whenever I'm nigh.
Tho' I talk all day long, I'm as mute as a fish,
And tho' wanting all things have nothing to wish.
I'm as red as a rose, yet as black as a crow,
Am the friend of mankind, yet am every man's foe.
I'm a king and a beggar, a drab and a queen,
And while charming *all eyes*, am not fit to be seen.

VERSES

By the side of the stream that strays thro' the grove,
I met in a ramble the blithe God of love;
His bow o'er his shoulder was carelessly tied,
His quiver in negligence clank'd at his side;
A grasp-full of arrows he held to my view,
Each wing'd with a feather, that differ'd in hue.
This, fledg'd from the eagle, he smiling begun,
I aim at the heart that no danger will shun;
And this, from the peacock, all gaudy, array'd,
The breast of Sir Fopling is sure to invade:
When I aim at the prattler, who talks, void of wit,
My shaft in the plume of a parrot will hit;
And when I've a mind that the jealous should smart,
An owl-feather'd arrow will pierce through his heart.
For the youth in whom truth and fondness reside,
From the breast of a dove my dart is supply'd;
This I value the most:—and this 't was, I found,
From you, O my Delia, that gave me the wound.

TO THE HEAVENLY MISS ARABELLA
BLOOMVILLE

What proof shall I give of my passion,
 Or how shall I struggle with fate?
Arabella! since cards came in fashion,
 You've mark'd me an object of hate.

I'd have willingly fought with the devil,
 And grateful have been, to be slain,
For I suffer indefinite evil,
 And warble alone to complain.

Like a madman I scour o'er the vallies,
 Unobserv'd like a mite in a cheese,
For 'tis the criterion of malice
 To laugh at my efforts to please.

Now I snuff the fresh air of the morning,
 In a transport of sorrow—because
You treat me with flouting and scorning,
 But hold, it is time I should pause.

                                ENDYMION.

WRITTEN, IN THE CLOSE OF WINTER,

TO

A FRIEND,

JUST LEAVING A FAVOURITE RETIREMENT,
PREVIOUS TO SETTLING ABROAD.

Ere yet your footsteps quit the place
Your presence long hath deign'd to grace,
With soft'ning eye and heart deplore,
The conscious scenes, your own no more.

    When vernal clouds their influence show'r,
Expand the bud, and rear the flow'r,
Who to yond leafing grove will come,
Where the rath primrose loves to bloom,
And fondly seek, with heedful tread,
The forward floret's downy head?
Or, when the vi'let leaves the ground,
Scent the pure perfume breathing round?
The garden tribes that gladlier grew,
While cherish'd by your fost'ring view,
No more disclose their wonted hues,
No more their wonted sweets diffuse!

    Who first will spy the swallow's wing?
Or hear the cuckoo greet the spring?
Unmark'd shall then th'assiduous dove,
With ruffling plumage, urge his love;
Unnoted, though in lengthen'd strain,
The bashful nightingale complain!
O'er the wide heath who then delight,
Led by the lapwing's devious flight,
To see her run, and hear her cry,
Most clam'rous with least danger nigh!

Who, saunt'ring oft, will listless stay,
Where rusticks spread th' unwither'd hay,
And, o'er the field, survey askance
The wavy vapour quiv'ring dance?
Or, sunk supine, with musing eye,
Listen the hum of noon-day fly?
Or watch the bee from bell to bell,
Where shelter'd lilies edge the dell?
Or, mid the sultry heat reclin'd,
Beneath the poplar woo the wind?
While, to the lightest air that strays,
Each leaf its hoary side displays.

Who, drawn by nature's varying face,
O'er heav'n the gath'ring tempest trace?
Or, in the rear of sunny rain,
Admire the wide bow's gorgeous train,
Till, blended, all its tincts decay,
And the dimm'd vision fleets away,
In misty streams of ruddy glow,
That cast an amber shine below;
And, melting into ether blue,
The freshen'd verdure gild anew!

Who now ascend the upland lawn,
When morning tines the kindling dawn,
To view the goss'mer pearl'd with dew,
That glist'ring shoots each mingling hue?
Or mark the clouds in liveries gay
Precede the radiant orb of day?
Who, when his amplest course is run,
Wistful pursue the sinking sun?
To common eyes he vainly shines;
Unheeded rises, or declines!

In vain with saffron light o'erspread,
Yond summit lifts its verdant head,
Defining clear each whiten'd cote,
And tuft of copse, to eye remote;
While, down the side-long steep, each oak,
Outbraving still the wood-man's stroke,
Detains, athwart th' impurpling haze,
A golden glance of west'ring rays.

The rook-lov'd groves, and grange between;
Dark hedge-row elms, with meadows green;
The grey church, peeping half through trees;
Slopes waving corn, as wills the breeze;
The podding bean-field, strip'd with balks;
The hurdl'd sheep-fold; hoof-trod walks;
The road that winds aslant the down;
The yellow furze-brake; fallow brown;
The wind-mill's scarcely circling vane;
The villager's returning wain;
The orient window's crimson blaze,
Obtrusive flaring on the gaze;
The eager heifer's echoing low,
Far from her calf compell'd to go;
From topmost ash the throstle's lay,
Bidding farewell to parting day;
The dale's blue smokes that curling rise;
The toil-free hind that homeward hies;
The stilly hum from glimmering wood;
The lulling lapse of distant flood;
The whitening mist that widening spreads,
As winds the brook adown the meads;
The plank and rail that bridge the stream;
The rising full-moon's umber'd gleam,
'Twixt sev'ring clouds that, richly dight,
Let gradual forth her bright'ning light;
No more the onward foot beguile,
Where pollards rude protect the stile.

Whose look now scans the dusky sphere,
To note succeeding stars appear?
Who now the flushing dawn descries,
That upward streams o'er northern skies?
Or the wan meteor's lurid light,
That, headlong trailing, mocks the sight?

Mid the lush grass, who now require
The glow-worm's ineffectual fire?
Or catch the bells from distant vale,
That load by fits the fresh'ning gale,
Till flurry'd from her ivy'd spray,
The moping owl rewing her way?

When autumn sere the copse invades,
No more you haunt the wood-land glades,
To eye the change from bough to bough;
Or eddying leaf descending slow,
That, lighting near her calm retreat,
Prompts the shy hare to shift her seat;
Or, peering squirrel nimbly glean
Each nut that hung before unseen;
Or, flitting down from thistle born;
Or, glossy haw that crowds the thorn,
Whence, oft in saws, observers old
Portend the length of winter's cold!

Wak'd by the flail's redoubling sound,
When spangling hoar-frost crisps the ground,
No more forego bewild'ring sleep,
To climb with health yond airy steep!
When deep'ning snows oppress the plain
The birds no more their boon obtain;
The red-breast, hov'ring round your doors,
No more the stated mess implores!
Where all that needed found relief,
No tearful eye laments their grief;
No lenient hand dispels their pain;
Fainting they sue, yet sue in vain.

But though the scenes you now deplore,
With heart and eye, be your's no more;
Though now each long known object seem
Unreal, as the morning's dream;
You still with retrospective glance,
Or rapt in some poetic trance,
At will, may ev'ry charm renew;
Each smiling prospect still review:
Through mem'ry's power and fancy's aid,
The pictur'd phantoms ne'er shall fade.
And, oh! where'er your footsteps roam,
Where'er you fix your future home,
May joys attending crown the past,
And heav'n's best mansion be your last!

A SWISS DAY

FROM THE ALBUM OF THE INN AT ZURICH

'Tis Dawn, lovely Dawn! and the sky is all white,
  And the cattle on vale and on hill-side are lowing,
And the lake lies in vapour, half morning, half night,
  And the breeze through the tops of the pine-groves
    is blowing;
And the vineyards are shaking the dew from their leaves,
  And down in the valley the village roofs shine,
And the doves are all rustling their wings in the eaves,
  And the Earth and the Heaven are cool, lovely, divine.

'Tis Morning, rich Morning! The yagers are out,
  And the rifles are ringing from valley to hill;
But the sun rises broad, and the horn and the shout
  Sink down, till we hear but the rush of the rill;
And, far up the mountain, the roebuck's brown troop
  Are seen, with the nostril spread out to the wind,
While the eagle above spreads his wings for a swoop,
  And the yagers toil on thro' the forest behind.

'Tis Noon, burning Noon! and the far village spire,
  And the peaks of the mountain, are arrows of flame,
And the air is a fever, the sunbeam a fire,
  And the deer, like the hunter, are weary and tame;
And the yagers by fountain and pine-tree are spread,
  Where the smoke of their meal curls up thro' the trees,
And the shepherd is slumbering in chalet and shed,
  And the fainting earth longs for the shower and the breeze.

'Tis Eve, balmy Eve! and above the hush'd world,
  Like a mother's red cheek o'er her soft-sleeping child,
On the East, with her pinion of crimson unfurl'd,
  The twilight is stooping, sweet, dewy, and mild;
And the planet of Eve looks on mountain and lake,
  Like a centinel spirit just glancing from heaven:
Oh, thus may we life and its trials forsake,
  And the hour of our parting be calm as this Even!

NAPOLEON

FROM THE ALBUM AT THE GREAT ST. BERNARD

Upon these snows the Despot trod,
The less than man, the would-be God!
Enough; let scornful history tell
Or how he rose, or how he fell:
How with the shipwreck sinks the surge,
What fire consumes the gory scourge,
What more than man's concentred hate
Pursues the murderer to his fate.
Enough;—here trod the homicide,
Here roll'd his legion's brazen tide;
Upon this mount the thunder-cloud
Shook o'er the vales the fiery shroud,
Rush'd on the pale Italian's throne,
And blazed, till prince and priest were gone.

Still onward swept thy sanguine tide,
Till blood with blood was purified;
Till Europe own'd HIS mightier will,
Who bids the ocean's wrath be still.
Then came, at last, thy judgment-hour,
Burst on thy march the icy shower,

Against the banner and the mail
Uprose the blast, uprose the hail,
Till all was done, and thou a slave,
A den thy realm, thy throne a grave!

ÆTNA

FROM THE ALBUM IN THE FRANCISCAN CONVENT AT
THE FOOT OF MOUNT ÆTNA

King of the Hills! was never king
  So throned and crown'd as thou.
A hundred forests' living ring,
  An ocean's azure flow,
    A kingdom, make thy royal zone,
    Thou King of nature's noblest throne!

Upon thy brow that white tiar
  Has lain six thousand years.
First-born of time! there's not a star
  In yonder heaven that rears
    On midnight's brows its fiery horn,
    Has seen the twilight of thy morn.

Earth's thrones have vanish'd like a dream,
  Earth's mightiest sunk in dust;
Wild whirl'd down time's returnless stream,
  Lyre, laurel, sceptre, bust;
    Sunk all alike, heart, hope, and name:—
    While thou, old king, art still the same!

Upon thy brow, Moor, Goth, and Greek,
  Have fix'd the wondering eye,
Watching thy awful splendours break
  Like morning on the sky;
    Or trembling at the thunder-roar
    From thy red heart's unfathom'd core.

There Homer from his galley gazed;
  As on the midnight tide
Along thy solemn shores it mazed:
  And down thy burning side
    Troop'd forms of immortality
    In vision on his dazzled eye.

There, by his charger, Hannibal
  Stood gazing on thy brow,
Thought of the Roman's fire-girt wall,
  The Alps' embattled snow,
    And saw in thy undying flame
    The emblem of the hero's fame.

The turban'd son of Mahomet
  Beheld thee o'er the wave!
Swore his hot lance in blood to whet,
  Till Europe was a grave,
    Hail'd Ætna as his battle sign,
    And swept the land in flames like thine.

And there the Crown-giver, the King
  Who sat on Europe's throne!
The rushing of whose Eagle's wing
  Bade kingdoms be undone.
    Napoleon, fix'd his infant eye,
    And there learn'd all things,—but to die!

He, too, is gone, ambition-curst;
  He fills an exile's grave:
But thou art glorious as at first;
  Thy grove, thy purple wave,
    Thy vineyard-wreath, are lovely all:
    Earth's pillar; but with Earth to fall!

ON THE WRECK OF A BRIG OFF DUNWICH

The hurricane roar'd through the starless night;
  Waves leap'd, as the mountains high;
And the sea-bird scream'd in his wild affright:
  Loud rose the sailor's cry!

And when the dim morn from the lowering east
  Broke o'er the storm-clad sea,
It was only to show Death's havoc-feast,
  On the day of his jubilee!

I heard in that morn the dire shout of distress
  Ring sharp from the parting deck;
And from Walberswick harbour to Orford ness,
  The beach was strewn with wreck!

I wander'd alone on the echoing shore,
  While the waves of the troubled bay,
Sent up to the heaven their angry roar,
  Like madden'd beasts of prey!

And I saw, as I turn'd, the dishevell'd hair
  Stream wildly on the gale;
And I heard the horrible cry of despair,
  And the mother's fearful wail,—

As she rush'd, in the strength of her agony, past,
  Like a wretch whose hope was gone;
And I heard her groans in the mocking blast,
  And her shriek— 'My son! my son!'

She knelt on the beach, and her hands on high
  Were thrown; and her lips apart,
Her pallid brow, and her frantic eye,
  Told the doom of a broken heart!

She gazed on the wreck that was floating near,
 Where she saw, on the heaving billow,
With the scatter'd shrouds for its rocking bier,
 And the foam of the sea for its pillow,—

She saw the corse of her son!—the sight
 Gave a pang to her bursting heart,
That sank 'neath the withering deadly blight,
 Which may come, but ne'er depart!

The next huge wave, in its giant strength,
 Threw the corse at the mother's feet,
With the sea-weed wrapp'd o'er its ghastly length,
 A cold, cold winding-sheet.

I saw the sad mother trembling stand—
 Methinks I see her now,
As she, shuddering, slowly pass'd her hand
 O'er the dead man's icy brow.

She shed no tear, and she heaved no sigh,
 But she stood as though the dire
And horrible glare of his unclosed eye
 Had sear'd her heart, like fire!

When the stay of our earthly joy is past,
 All wreck'd on the shoal of time;
Oh! where shall the soul her anchor cast
 In this world of woe and crime?

There *is* a haven, to which her bark
 May steer from the tempest's strife,
And rest, as of old did the sacred ark,
 On the Ararat of life!

Yes! the wounded heart must seek for health,
 At a spring which faileth never;
That glideth and giveth its priceless wealth,
 By the throne of God, for ever!

SONG

What is this sentimental love—
   This spell of the romantic mind,
Whose flimsy texture fancy wove
   Too weak th' impassion'd heart to bind!

Does it from nature spring? Ah! no;
   Nature the airy form denies—
Is it by reason bred? If so,
   Why always hid from reason's eyes?

Is it a quick inspiring flame
   That animates with love the heart?
No— its cold dictates strangely aim
   A mental fervor to impart.

Dull apathy, or frozen age,
   The phantom conjur'd first to view;
The policy or envious rage
   Of those who ne'er true rapture knew.

Away! no more my thoughts detain,
   Illusive, visionary sprite!
May love's warm stream thro' ev'ry vein
   Roll gay desire and fond delight.

And may the youth whose sparkling eyes
   For love and mutual bliss were sent,
Ne'er damp my ardours as they rise,
   With the chill clouds of sentiment.

When howling winds and louring skies
The light untimber'd bark surprize,
　　Near Orkney's boisterous seas;
The trembling crew forget to swear,
And bend their knees, unused to prayer,
　　To ask a little ease.

For ease the Turk ferocious prays,
For ease the barbarous Russe,—for ease,
　　Which P—— could ne'er obtain,
Which Bedford lack'd amidst his store,
And liberal Clive with mines of ore,
　　Oft bade for—but in vain.

For not the liveried troops that wait
Around the mansions of THE GREAT,
　　Can keep, my friend! aloof
Fear; that attacks the mind by fits,
And Care that like a raven flits,
　　Around the lordly roof.

O well is he; to whom kind Heaven
A decent competence has given,
　　Rich in the blessing sent;
He grasps not anxiously at more,
Dreads not to use his little store,
　　And fattens on content.

O well is he! for life is lost,
Amid a whirl of passions tost;
   Then why, dear Jack, should man,
Magnanimous ephemera! stretch
His views beyond the narrow reach
   Of his contracted span?

Why should he from his country run,
In hopes beneath a foreign sun
   Serener hours to find?
Was never man in this wild chase?
Who changed his nature with his place,
   And left himself behind.

For winged with all the lightning's speed
Care climbs the bark, care mounts the steed,
   An inmate of the breast;
Nor Barca's heat, nor Zembla's cold,
Can drive from that pernicious hold,
   The too tenacious guest.

They, whom no anxious thoughts annoy,
Grateful the present hour enjoy,
   Nor seek the next to know;
To lighten ev'ry ill they strive,
Nor, ere misfortune's hand arrive,
   Anticipate the blow.

Something must ever be amiss,
Man has his joys; but perfect bliss
   Lives only in the brain;
We cannot all have all we want,
And chance unask'd to THIS may grant
   What THAT has begg'd in vain.

WOLF rush'd on death in manhood's bloom,
PAULET crept slowly to the tomb;
   Here BREATH, there FAME was given,
And that wise power who weighs our lives
By contras and by pers contrives
   To make the balance even.

To THEE she gave two piercing eyes,
A body— just of Tydeus' size,
   A judgment sound and clear,
A mind, with various science fraught,
A liberal soul, a threadbare coat,
   And forty pounds a year.

To ME, one eye, not over good,
Two sides, that to their cost have stood,
   A ten years' hectic cough.
Aches, stitches, all the numerous ills
That swell the dev'lish Doctors' bills,
   And sweep poor mortals off:

A coat more bare than thine, a soul
That spurns the croud's malign controul,
   A fix'd contempt of wrong;
Spirits above affliction's pow'r,
And still to charm the lonely hour,
   WITH NO INGLORIOUS SONG!

Ah, well-a-day!
It is not now the month of May,
Yet let us all be gay,
    Ah well-a-day!

    Yes, we will sing
The praise of every living thing,
And for each other we will bring
    The flow'rs of spring.

    Ah, well-a-day!
I must not sport with virgin play,
I'm married, as they say,
    Ah, well-a-day!

When you are absent all looks drearly,
   When you are absent I am sad,
Because I love my Henry dearly,
   When he is with me I am glad.

O then, unless you wish to grieve me,
   No more desert my circling arms;
It breaks my heart that you should leave me,
   The lord, the master of my charms.

ODE TO SENTIMENT

What art thou, Sentiment, unkind,
That thus within the ruby-tinctured wave
Of lovers' hearts dost love to lave
Thy fangs, that rend the poet's trembling mind
With rapturous, oh! and danger-breathing thrills?
Dwell'st thou on rugged rocks, or high-topp'd hills,
Or art thou to the verdant vales confin'd?
I see thee floating o'er the primrose ground,
Thy brows with garlands of mimosa bound
And myrtle-mingling leaves!
Quivering at thy approach, my tear-stain'd lids
Are *oped*, as cruel genius bids,
And quick my palpitating bosom heaves!
My senses trill!
By mazy rill,
That seems all form'd of lovers' tears,
The poet of the living lyre appears!
He strikes with dulcet hand the chords,
Singing sighs and wounding words;
And scatters from his pictur'd harp
Spiry flames and arrows sharp.
Above, below,
They seem to go;
Where threaded sinews seem to start,
Charged with each—a lover's heart!
And deeply drink my heart's best—Oh!
His beamy eyes of sky-ey blue,
Like sapphires in their caves of mossy hue,
Or vernal hyacynths of azure true,
Baptiz'd by Zephyr's hands in flower-extracted dew.
He comes!—Oh! silence with thy ermine glove,
Hush every sound—but that of him I love;
With sandals of the thistle's crown,
That feathery floats along the down,
Ye balmy-breathing breezes, move.
Hush every sound but *his voice* whom I love,

And oh! be *cobweb Contemplation* wove
O'er his luxurious lyre,
To notes of soft desire,
That never tire!   [wishes thrown,
Be wreaths of tender thoughts and wandering
Mix'd with unfaded roses newly blown!
His trembling ardors he infuses,
Extract from the melting muses;
And softer far,
Than from the reed-woven jar
Florentine oil in pearly-dropping oozes.
Oh! his wild notes entrance my soul,
Yet ah! my transports to controul,
Iron Remembrance comes; and copper Care,
And Sorrow's steely form, *upon my soul*,
Rouses the *red Remorse*;
Ah! cruel curse
My passion fades,
Duty pervades
My every sense; my bosom's Lord appears,
Prudence *nears*,
Eyes and ears,
Your bosom's Lord obey!
Hush'd be your murmurs, heart too tender!
Thou to luxuriant Love must *not* surrender—
Let Della Crusca thee seduce no more;
But to thy conjugal affection true,
Fly for ever from the view
Of eyes, like *spring-born* Periwinkle's, blue!
They fade like stars away;
While I, deep sighing, say,
What is pleasure, what is May?
Love o'er my couch has strewn each sweet,
Love has sigh'd, trembling at my feet:
He has indeed,
But o'er the mead
He flies; and Sensibility doth linger
Only with cruel, quivering finger,
To say—Henceforth Matilda shuns
Crusca, and all his wilderness of suns.

SONNETS

THE CALM

The winds are hush'd — once more the sky's serene,
  The lightning spent — the roaring thunders cease;
Returning sunbeams gild the past'ral scene —
  And all around is happiness and peace.

The rain-drop quivers on the verdant spray,
  The shrubs again their lovely bloom renew,
The vocal choirs resume their broken lay —
  And Nature smiles through pearly gems of dew!

Who can the pleasures of the village tell,
  When from their huts the rural tribes advance?
Who, while no curfew sounds the evening knell,
  With nimble footsteps trace the mazy dance —
While songs of humour, innocence and glee,
  Bespeak and bless the Sons of Liberty!

SONNET

When sorrow's humblest haunts reflect the beam
    That patient virtue scatters o'er the plain,
No wanton zephyr curls the languid stream,
    No melting woodlark wakes the warbled strain.

For me, alas! beset with storms of woe,
    Where plaintive ecchoes die upon the gale,
May the still voice of agony bestow,
    The softest requiem to the rustic vale.

O! my lov'd Henry! shouldst thou ever hear
    How feebly flows the meditated lay,
While the pale moonshine gilds the checquer'd sphere;
    Thou might'st again the distant theme display,
Might'st drop th' appropriate plaudit of a tear,
    And whisper sweetness to the charms of May.

DARKNESS

Oh! Darkness! hide me with thine ebon ray,
And let thy brown shade o'er my bosom drop,
Guard my sad bosom from the torch of day,
And bid thy chills my hurrying pulses stop;
While in thy glimmering gloom I gladly wrap
My temples, and attune the soul-sad lay!
Reclining on the meadow's breathing crop
Of bos-befriending flower-besprinkled hay;
Or 'neath the verdant shade of cypress stop,
To hear sweet Philomel salute the May.
Come, gentle Darkness, in thy veil of jet
Enwreathe me, votary of the moist-eyed muse!
So in thy raven robe I may forget
Pearlina! and drink deep oblivious dews.

THE MOPSTICK

Straight remnant, of the spiry birchen bough,
    That o'er the streamlet wont perchance to quake
Thy many twinkling leaves, and, bending low,
    Beheld thy white rind dancing on the lake—

How doth thy present state, poor stick! awake
    My pathos—for, alas! even stript as thou
May be my beating breast, if e'er forsake
    Philisto this poor heart; and break his vow.

So musing on I fare, with many a sigh,
    And meditating then on times long past,
To thee, lorn pole! I look with tearful eye,
    As all beside the floor-soil'd pail thou'rt cast,
And my sad thoughts, while I behold thee twirl'd,
Turn on the twistings of this troublous world.

ELEGIES

Where slow meand'ring thro' the verdant plain,
  Yon rill with murm'ring melancholy flows,
Contiguous to the spot where, hapless swain!
  Young William's straw-clad cottage once arose.

Lost in incomprehensibility
  Of those dire pangs which rent his tortured breast,
When on his death-bed laid with many a sigh,
  His soul departed, leaving me unblest.

I gaily hasten'd to the well-known spot,
  Where I had oft partaken curds and tart,
Untir'd by repetition, 'twas my lot,
  To share the dainties of his dairy's art.

The slipp'ry butter which in daily course,
  Was by his pretty sister Mary made,
Ah happy days, but now distress, remorse,
  In sad perfection my torn thoughts invade.

For gone alas! are this once blissful pair,
  And anguish only now remains for me;
He left a monkey, that my griefs shall share,
  And mourn the season I no more shall see.

CONJUGAL LOVE

AN ELEGY

If aught of bliss sincere hath e'er been giv'n,
  To those who dwell so far beneath the skies,
That bliss, which makes on earth a present heav'n,
  Can only from the purest passions rise.

Say, do not storms uproot the lofty oak,
  That crowns with majesty the mountain's brow;
While lowly shrubs escape the thunder's stroke,
  And wave their verdure in the vale below?

Say, does that soil whose bosom gold contains,
  From its rich lap in more profusion throw,
Or sweeter flow'rs than scent unpillag'd plains,
  Where baneful gold hath ne'er been taught to glow?

Say, does that haughty bird whose gaudy train
  Attracts the full gaze of the splendid day,
Pour from the heart so soothing, sweet a strain,
  As modest Philomela's melting lay?

Ambition, av'rice, and the pomp of pride,
  Seductive oft, may lure unheedful eyes,
But ne'er can tempt my right-on foot aside;
  These who pursue, will ne'er obtain the prize.

Remote from envy, far from madding strife,
  I nothing want, of competence possess'd;
Amid the scenes of mild domestic life,
  I'll seek, by blessing others, to be bless'd.

Be mine the first, the most endearing care,
    That nought may e'er disturb my Delia's joy:
Whate'er to her could cause the lightest fear,
    Would instant all my happiness destroy.

For her I'd wake e'en at the glimpse of dawn,
    And blithsome at the heavy plough would toil;
Anticipating, e'er my wish'd return,
    The ready welcome of an heart-felt smile.

When autumn o'er our fields her produce spreads,
    And vying reapers bend in adverse rows;
With pleasure she the yellow landscape treads,
    And wipes the dews of labour from their brows.

Should sickness e'er molest my menial train,
    With lenient hand she'd ev'ry grief assuage;
Her sympathy would draw the sting of pain,
    Revive the young, and charm e'en wayward age.

Should some kind friend frequent our humble shed,
    With studious ease she'd grace the frugal board;
Before our guest her rural treasures spread,
    Nor boast a treat but what our grounds afford.

Should some bewilder'd trav'ler as he strays,
    Protection seek beneath our shelt'ring roof,
For him she'll make the cheerful hearth to blaze,
    Of hospitality the promptest proof.

The hallow'd raptures of the bridal bed,
    When, first entranc'd, we seal'd our mutual vow,
Transport less poignant through the bosom sped,
    Than yields the fond delight that fills us now.

Ah, speak, my Delia, thy o'erflowing heart,
    When, cradl'd in thine arm, the tender boy,
With filial smile doth first begin t' impart,
    He knows his mother, source of all his joy!

Or, when around my knees the infant band,
   In clamb'ring contest seek the envy'd kiss,
Impetuous, each extends the pleading hand,
   T'assert his claim, and all obtain the bliss;

While we, in sportive contest, strive to trace,
   In which each parent's semblance most prevails,
Their father's vigour and thy winning grace,
   In varied mixture o'er each feature steals.

Oft, when their little tongues but ill can tell
   The sprightly fancies in their brain that rise;
With keen attention thou explor'st them well,
   And read'st the meaning in their speaking eyes.

'Delightful task, the tender thought to rear,
   To teach the young idea how to shoot!'
To prune each impulse that a vice might bear,
   And tend with fos'tring hand the rip'ning fruit!

When tott'ring lambkins, from the searching air,
   Unable yet the fresh world to sustain,
Demand the fold, be their's the tender care,
   Nor will they hear the suff'rers bleat in vain.

When timid red-breast, pinch'd by taming cold,
   Enters our friendly cot in search of food;
Be their's the joy to make the stranger bold,
   And learn the luxury of doing good.

Thus, with their op'ning minds our pleasures spread,
   While they in all that's just and gen'rous thrive,
Till autumn's mellowing hues our days o'ershade,
   Then in our scyons we'll again revive.

Fond mem'ry then shall make us feel anew,
   Those happy hours, when you first touch'd my heart;
Recall each dear idea to our view,
   When you that wounded, smiling eas'd the smart.

Then, in my boys, some lovely maid I'll woo,
   Whose virtues, and whose form, resemble thine;
While, in your girls, shall pay his court to you,
   Some honest youth, whose bosom glows like mine.

And when, at length, draws on the gloom of death,
   We'll praise our God for all his blessings giv'n;
In gentle slumber yield our easy breath,
   And, both transported, wake to bliss in heav'n.

EPITAPHS

FROM THE *LITERARY GAZETTE*

(ELEVEN EPITAPHS)

POETRY

ORIGINAL POETICAL VARIETIES

Bath, Oct. 1822.

Mr. Editor,—In my rambles about this neighbourhood, I collected the following verses from the tombstones of different church-yards. Some of the most whimsical, though nearly effaced, are still to be found in the cemetery of a rather considerable town on the high road from London to Bristol, and are probably the production of the same goose-quill; but whether wielded by the sexton, clerk, or even parson of the parish, I could not learn: all I discovered upon the subject was, that some of them have been inscribed a good many years ago, apparently enough before the dawn of our present most wonderful poetical era.

I remain, Mr. Editor, &c.&c. *Viator.*

That thou would'st pity take I humbly pray,
O Lord, on this my wretched lump of clay—
A broken pitcher do not cleave in twain,
But let me rise, and be myself again.

———————————

I went and listed in the tenth Hussars,
And gallopped with them to the bloody wars—
'Die for your Sovereign,—for your country die!'
To earn such glory feeling rather shy,
Snug I slipped home; but Death soon sent me off
After a struggle with the hooping cough.

Here lye in the blessed hope of a joyful resurrection
The bodies of   Prudence ⎞
               Martha ⎬ Wilcox
              and   ⎟
              Obadiah ⎠
    Aged one—two—and three years.
       Three children small
       Composed my all—
       But envious death
       Has stopped their breath,
       And left, d'ye see,
       My wife and me,
       Above the knee,
       In sorrow's slough—
       To help us through
       The Lord alone,
       Who hears our groan,
       Knows how and when!
            AMEN, AMEN.

There down at Katherines*I kept a school,
Vended small wares, caught rats, and carded wool;
My wife excelled in making British wine,
But she's alive and is no longer mine;
For I am dead and she won't follow—
I can no longer whoop and hollow—
Reader, if thou dost wish to know
The name of him here lying low,
Look down upon this stone, and see
Wilcox conjoined with Timothy.

*A village near Bath-Easton.

Tread soft, good friends, least you should spring a
      mine!
I was a workman in the powder line.
Of true religion I possessed no spark
Till Christ, he pleased to stop my gropings dark.
The Rev'rend Vicar seconded the plan,
[A temperate, holy, charitable man,
Who left the foxes to enjoy their holes,
And never hunted aught but human souls]
To this Director's care 'twas kindly given
To point my spirit, bolt upright, to heaven.

Here lies John Adams who received a thump
Right in the forehead from the Parish pump
Which gave him his quietus in the end,
For many Doctors did his case attend.

Shadowed with doubts, and agonized with fears,
I float to God upon a tide of tears!—
Afar the Beacon!—yet I see it shine—
Despond, avaunt—Faith makes the haven mine.

In Memory of
Sarah Palmer, who departed this life, March 16,
1782, in the 91 year of her age—leaving children,
grand children, great grand children, and treble
grand children, 166—

By his kind help, who sits on Heaven's throne,
I reached the reverend age of ninety-one—
At eighty-seven, I had a broken shin—
At eighty-nine, I halved my doze of gin,
And being come to ripe maturity,
Placed all my thoughts upon futurity;
Thinking I heard a blessed angel say,
Cherry, old Soul, pack up, and come away.

Hear from the tomb the warning voice of truth!
A lingering malady consumed my youth—
John Sims my name, a carpenter's my trade;
With half confessions, like a blushing maid,
To a famed Leech I humbly did apply,
Though no one knew the cause or reason why—
His sovereign cordials flowed for me in vain,
His pills procured me only change of pain—
So next I dragged my steps to Doctor Greedy,
Who made me ten times worse and still more needy.
Worn to a stump I sought the reverend Jay,
Not in the pill, but in the spir'tual way—
He cleansed my inward man, he heard my sigh,
Preached down my Quacks and taught me how to
    die.

To the Memory of
Thomas and Richard Fry
Stonemasons,

Who were crushed to death August the 25th, 1776,
by the slip-down of a wall they were in the act of
building. Thomas was aged 19—and Richard 21 years—
"They were lovely and pleasant in their lives, and in death
they were not divided.—Blessed are they who die in the
Lord, for their works follow them."

A sacred truth! now learn our awful fate!
Dear friends we were, first cousins, and what not—
To toil as masons was our humble lot;
As just returning from a house of call,
The Parson bade us set about his wall—
Flushed with good liquor, cheerfully we strove
To place big stones below, and big above—
We made too quick work—down the fabric came,
It crushed our vitals—people bawled out, Shame!
But we heard nothing—mute as fish we lay,
And shall lie sprawling till the judgment day—
From our misfortune this good moral know:
Never to work too fast, or drink too slow.

Near this Stone are deposited the mortal remains of Mrs.
Elinor Parkins, who kept the "Red Lion" in this town with
great credit more than 16 years.

Assigned by Providence to rule a Tap,
My days passed glibly—till an awkward rap,
Some way like bankruptcy, impelled me down;
But up I got again, and shook my gown
In gamesome gambols, quite as brisk as ever—*(Sic)*
Blithe as the lark, and gay as sunny weather—
Composed with creditors at five in pound,
And frolicked on till laid in holy ground.
The debt of nature must, you know, be paid—
No trust from her—God grant extent in aid.

Part of the epitaph of a school-mistress, who died, strange to say, on 1st April 1824. She was accomplished to

Solve a conundrum; or compose a riddle;
Play on the flute, the bagpipes, and the fiddle;
Adore the Bible, and eschew romances,
Study Geography, and tell where France is;
So wide, so general her teaching powers,
She taught her donkey to declare the hours....

. . . .

She could have taught the veriest owl that hoots,
To act and thrive as well as Mistress Coutts.

———————

Here lies my dear Wife,
A most fidgetty Jade,
Worth nothing in Sun-shine
But something in Shade.

———————

Here lies the body of Lucinda Howard,
Who neither ugly was, nor false, nor froward;
But good and pretty, as this verse declares,
And sav'd from drowning by his Reverence Squares.
But small the 'vantage, for she scarce was *dried*,
Before she made a sad faux pas—and DIED.

Ye who the merits of the dead revere,
Who hold misfortune sacred, genius dear,
Regard this tomb, where Lady Barton's name
Solicits kindness with a double claim!
Tho' nature gave her, and thro' science taught
The fire of fancy, and the reach of thought;
Severely, doom'd to suffer grief's extreme,
She pass'd, in madd'ning pain, life's fev'rish dream;
While rays of genius only serv'd to shew
The thick'ning horror and exalt her woe.
Ye walls that eccho'd to her frantic moan,
Guard the due records of this grateful stone!
Strangers to her, enamour'd of her lays,
This fond memorial to her talents raise.
For this the ashes of a Fair require
Who touch'd the tend'rest notes of pity's lyre;
Who join'd pure faith to strong poetic powers,
Who in reviving reason's lucid hours
Sought in one book her troubled mind to rest,
And rightly deem'd the book of God the best.

ON A DEAD GOLDFINCH

Poor little bird that died one day,
As kings and other people may!
Ah! what would gentle Henry say
To find your life thus past away?

But Henry, O my pretty dear!
Is gone far off, and is not here.
Therefore does Arabella fear,
He is not overmuch sincere.

When next the morn begins to rise,
Again thou wilt not ope thine eyes,
And thus my faithless Henry flies,
And leaves me looking at the skies.

Begone then balmy zephyrs, go,
And let my cruel Henry know
That on this fruitful earth below,
No other man could use me so!

My Goldfinch died—how did he dare,
To leave me lost in deep despair?
Then let each maiden, sunk in care,
Of Lovers such as mine, beware.

FONTHILL AND LANSDOWN POEMS

ON A FIRST VIEW

OF

FONTHILL ABBEY,

AUGUST 21st, 1822.

The mighty master wav'd his wand, and lo!
On the astonish'd eye the glorious show
Bursts, like a vision! SPIRIT OF THE PLACE,
Has the Arabian wizard, with his mace
Smitten the barren downs far onward spread,
And bade th' enchanted Palace tow'r instead?
Bade the dark woods their solemn shades extend?
High to the clouds yon spiry tow'r ascend?
And starting from th' umbrageous avenue,
Spread the rich pile magnificent to view?
   Enter—from this arch'd portal, look again,
Back, on the lessening woods and distant plain.
Ascend the steps—the high and fretted roof
Is woven by some Elfin hand aloof,
Whilst from the painted windows' long array,
A mellow'd light is shed, as not of day.
How gorgeous all! Oh never may the spell
Be broken, that array'd those radiant forms so well.
W.L. BOWLES

This poem, published in 1824, continues for a further 36 pages.

FONTHILL

Stupendous Art! whose mighty remnants gild,
Those Climes and Scenes, once with thy glories fill'd;
Those Climes, alas! where now Barbarians stray,
Or Despots rule, and trembling Slaves obey;
But still, where struggling, panting to be free,
Man strives to burst the bonds of tyranny;—
Stupendous Art! I hail thee on thy throne,
The proud Acropolis, thy favor'd zone;
Where rear'd in all thy grace, magnificence,
Unrivall'd soars, and awes the lab'ring sense:
Yes, Architecture, there thy crown is hung,
There thy chief witchery, there thy beauties flung;
Revolving ages thence have sung thy praise,
And o'er thy forehead shook the victor bays;
Announc'd thy triumphs, from all rivals won,
While Fame's wide trump resounds the Parthenon.

JOHN JEFFERSON

FONTHILL

Man and his works!   The meteor's gleam,
The sun-flash on a winter stream,
A vision seen in sleep, that gives
Of gladness more than aught which lives,
A palace from a splendid cloud
Formed, while the wind is rising loud,
A bubble on the lake, a cry
Heard sad from sea when storms are high,
Ways made through air by wild birds's wings,
Are sure and well established things;
Man and his works! words writ on snow
Are emblem of them both below:
Stars dropt from heaven to darkness thrown,
A moment light—and all is gone.

See, Art has cast her spell to check
Man's greatness ere it goes to wreck;
Here, Turner, with a wizard's power,
Has fixed in splendour tree and tower;
And bravely from oblivion won,
A landscape steeped in dew and sun.
A grove, a shepherd, sheep, a rill,
Towers seen o'er all—behold Fonthill!
Where, like a saint embalmed and shrined,
Long worshiped Beckford dozed and dined;
Strayed through that wood, strolled by that brook
Ate much—thought little—wrote a book;
Tattled with titled dames and sighed
In state like any prince, and died.
And that's Fonthill! things of high fame
Less lovely are in look than name—
Spots bright in song and fair in story
Glow far less lustrous than their glory:
Historians' heroes, poets' lasses,
Shine glorious through Fame's magic glasses,
Who in rude war, or rapture's hour,
Had no such heart-inspiring power.

So fares it with Fonthill, which proud
Shoots there in lustre to the cloud;
Give fame its portion, art its share,
And all the rest is empty air.
No longer, through the lighted hall,
Its lord at midnight leads the ball;
Nor, dancing 'mid its dazzling rooms,
Young jewelled beauty shakes her plumes;
Nor bards are there, glad to rehearse
A rich man's praise in trembling verse;
Nor shrewder souls who breathe rich wines
In laughter when their landlord shines:
All, all are gone—the green grass sward,
On jewelled belle and beau and bard
And man of rank, grows long and green,
Nor seems to know that such have been.
The tower that rose so proud and fair,
Hath left its station in mid air;
While in its place the sunbeam flings
Its glory down—the skylark sings:
O'er the wide space usurped by vain
Man, Nature hath resumed her reign.

So, hath it been, and will be still
With all, as well as proud Fonthill.
Where's Cicero's villa, Caesar's hall!
Attila's hut, Alaric's pall?
The throne of iron whence late flew forth
Napoleon's words which shook the earth!
Men, glorious men, where are they gone,
Who ruled and fooled and sinned and shone?
And women who, like babes in strings,
Led mighty earls and conquering kings?
They lie beneath our feet—we tread,
Regardless, o'er the illustrious dead!
The dust which we shake from our shoe,
Once breathed and lived and loved.   Adieu!
Dames with their charms, bards with their laurel—
Read ye who run, and sigh the moral.

FONTHILL ABBEY, WILTS,
SEAT OF W. BECKFORD, ESQ.

IN JULY 1827.

Softly we tread these tangled slopes;
Sad wild shrubs sigh o'er blasted hopes,
And perfumes from neglected flowers
Breathe of these once Elysian bowers.
So Beauty fades—so flit the brightest hours.

All that unbounded wealth could claim—
High genius and an honour'd name—
Were here enshrined. Rich works of Art
To thrill and warm the coldest heart,
All gathered here—like shadows to depart!

Thou Vathek in thy vast enchanted Hall
Didst Monarch sit o'er slaves in abject thrall.
The Nobles of the land, its plumed Head,
Bow'd with an wful superstitious dread.
Such talismanic power was in thy sway,
That the whole world would deepest homage pay:
The Arbiter of all that gives a zest
To this life's pleasures on thy throne confest!

Why on this cold and lonely waste
Was this his gorgeous Abbey placed!
To frown with scorn upon the towers
Of Wardour—Arundel's fair bowers,
Here friendship flourish'd and sweet peace;
Yon Hermit little knew of these.
The proud Plebeian could not brook
The high-soul'd Noble's open look,
And sought at length in life drear wane
To fly his sated fancy's pain.

His air-built Castle sank to nought,
When gold its transient treasures bought.
His Dwarf and grooms in gothic state
No longer tend that Abbey gate.

Dim had become the far-West gold;
　　The slaves he once had own'd
Burst from their chains' despotic hold,
　　Wherein they long had groan'd.

Broken the spell! A motley crowd
　　Flock from all countries round:
Where silence reign'd, now voices loud
　　Profane this fairy ground.

The lofty Tower and gilded halls
　　Are throng'd from morn till eve;
Art's glorious works that grace those walls
　　All doom'd each niche to leave.

The master-mind is working still—
　　The Painter's, Sculptor's eye
Has deftly with consummate skill
　　The choicest gems laid by

To deck some lowlier hermitage,
　　Where long the rill of life
Flow'd murmuring on. The Sacred Page
　　Quell'd not his spirit's strife.

Man's bright creations soon must fade,
Soon sink in dark oblivion's shade,
A crash was heard at midnight hour—
Low in the dust that lofty Tower!
Broken the spell! Behold that mass!
So swift away earth's glories pass!
Two turrets, all that now remain,
In sadness o'erlook the plain!

Oh, Beckford! could no inward conscious shame
Prevail—still wouldst thou to the world proclaim
The scene of all thy gloomy selfish days,
And on a distant hill a watch-tower raise,
To view those turrets crumbling in decay,
Mocking thy grace at evening's parting ray!
Thou too art fall'n—thy tinsel glory set,
We pay thy name at least a willing debt;
Would that thy honour'd Sire's well-earn'd renown
Had shone thy life to grace—thy death to crown!
O'er hours this gifted Anchorite had pass'd
Let Charity her kindly mantle cast;
The Judge will on his awful Day decide
Our brother's state; 'tis ours his faults to hide.
A Beacon still for wealth and genius to behold:
The Haven is not gain'd by talent or by gold!

E.K.

Jaulnah, Bombay, July 1856

FONTHILL ABBEY

From verdant scenes of groves and woody hills
Of lofty eminence, where stately firs
And giant oaks, and aspens gray, defy
The patting anger of the blast, and wave
Their dewy foliage in the breath of morn,
When first the spiry boast of Sarum's pile
Cradles the infant ray of light—
                                        Or when
They swing their leafy branches in the breeze
What time the fiery orb descends apace,
And shoots his glory through the checkered pines
That crest the Beacon-cliff—a sacred spot
Of deep and silent sorrow, for it looks
As if some dear, departed friend slept there—
    And from th' unruffled crystal of the lake
Below, the deep, mysterious, old remain
Of silenced craters, of volcanoes dire
That once disturbed the soil, and shook around
The feverish land—but now a watery plain,
Pellucid and so smooth! with sedgy banks
Of lively green or pebbly margins, where,
Happy and conscious of their freedom, play
The water-fowls, and mix their clamorous notes
With the deep groanings of the labouring wheel
That robs the Naiads in the lonely glen
Of the clear treasure of their silver urns,
To heave and send it upwards to the hill
That swells aloft—

And from the bowers
Of various Edens, all perfumed with shrubs
Of foreign growth, all speckled with bright flowers
Of passing odorous scent—above the clouds—
Solemn in gothic majesty—the ABBEY starts
In full display upon the sapphire vault
Of purest air!...

        Thus, so they feign, sublime,
'Twixt heaven and earth, by magic art, arose
The mountain-son of Japhet, huge and bold,
To prop the Spheres.

        No Gorgon's direful face,
No secret talisman, nor fairy wand,
These wonders wrought;—but Genius, Taste, and Power
Combined, conceived the whole, and bade it rise
Magnificent—its bosom to contain
What plastic Nature and what skilful Art
Could e'er achieve.

        Here burst at once
Upon th' astonished sight, the rarest spoils
Of Eastern mines and of Peruvian ores—
The gold which Tagus in his waters rolls—
The shining sands of Famed Pactolus—and
All precious metals with more precious gems
Adorned—a world of weath—a radiant heaven
Of matchless beauties!—

Here the spotless vase
Of icy crystal vies with agate, stained
By Nature's fancy-hands; the ruby bright,
In crimson lightnings, flashes on the eye
Its living fires—the faint, the lovely amethyst,
That looks so like the swooning virgin's lips—
The sanguine stone, that spills the poisonous draught—
Celestial sapphires, verdant emeralds, all
Meet here.
   The Pallet too, on lofty walls,
Her tributary stores displays—the works
Of hands now clasped in the cold grasp of death,
Inimitable.....
   Through the blazoned halls,
The storied galleries and princely rooms,
A bright galaxy of heraldic stars,
Long lines of noblest ancestry, declare
Who planned, who raised the splendid mansion, where,
Above the puny jarrings of the world,
Above the strife for glory and for power,
Wrapt in his cloak of learning and of wit,—
A mind of fire, a deeply feeling heart,—
The founder stands aloft—a stranger to our sphere!

THOUGHTS SUGGESTED
IN MR BECKFORD'S PARK
THE DAY AFTER HIS DECEASE.

The master is departed from his place—
Again by weeds each path shall be defiled:
The paradise that opened in the wild
Shall be obscured; yea, soon shall not a trace
Rest of that beauty art from nature drew:
Strokes that so well the master-artist knew!
The wild rose now shall wither in its bloom:
And the azalia droop as o'er a tomb!
Closed is the eye that watched them—cold the tongue
That praised—the hand that life around them flung.
The moss'd-roof grot shall open to the wind;
The green-sward path that led to solitude,
Of leafy haunts where meditation broods,
The thorn shall hide, and bramble unconfined.
The wilderness shall grow again, and all
The beautiful that like a coronal
Crowned the bare hills depart like a far dream,
The mind that cast its own reflection on
The Earth, and covered like a sunshine gleam,
Is vanished from its place—a light that shone.

Yet over all looks Summer's glorious eye,
As 'neath her glance no living thing could die!
So onward rolls the tendency of things,
The stream of life from its eternal springs.
A moment yet—and he who lingers here
Becomes the mourned, and draws the transient tear:
Leaves this loved scene by years familiar made,
Himself forgot—his memory a shade!

JOHN EDMUND READE.

FONTHILL SALE
The sale gave rise to numerous jeux d'esprit, *and also to the following amusing skit, issued as a broadside and now extremely rare.*

FONTHILL SALE*

A Parody

Who has not heard of the Sale at Fonthill,
With its bijou the brightest that earth ever gave;
Its pictures and books—and its knights of the quill
Who of all its attractions so ceaselessly rave?
Oh, to see it at midday, when warm o'er the HALL
Its full gathered splendour an autumn sun throws;
Ere the smug auctioneer to his seat in his stall
'Like a bride full of blushes' so smilingly goes:
And punctual to time without stoppage or stammer,
Reads his list of 'Conditions' and raises his hammer.

When gems, bronzes and paintings are gleaming half shewn
(Mr. Beckford's we mean—t'other half would not please, Sir)
From tables of ebony—rosewood—and one
Which they tell us belonged to the Prince of Borghese, Sir,
But *geese* we should be all we hear thus to hug
Since we know many come from the Prince of Humbug.
Then to see all the China from Nankin and Dresden,
The 'rare Oriental' and 'famed Japanese,'
Mixed with all kinds of trumpery, but recently pressed in,
Our judgements to dupe and our pockets to ease.
With bronzes and boxes—*chefs-d'œuvre* of skill,—
Made 'to order' they say for the sale at Fonthill.

---

* The chief part of this Fragment is in imitation, or rather parody, of the celebrated
description of the Vale of Cashmere, in Moore's 'Light of the Harem,' beginning:
  Who has not heard of the Vale of Cashmere

Here the music of bidding grows loud and more loud;
Here the *sweetener* is conning his hints for the day;
And here by the rostrum, apart from the crowd,
Billy Tims and his brethren are scribbling away
(Striving who shall bedaub Mr. Phillips the most)
Their puffs for the *Chronicle*, *Herald* and *Post*.
Let us pause ere we blame, for 'tis well understood,
Though some things are so-so, Harry's dinners are good,
And since paying and feeding the piper's no jest,
Sure they ought to play for him the tune he likes best.

Here a black-letter hero with rat-smelling air
Tipping winks full of meaning, squats down in his chair,
The veteran of many a Book-auction is he,
And he'll not be bamboozled we think, Mr. P.
If the item is genuine away goes his nod,
And if cheap is knocked down with ''Tis yours, Mr. Rodd,'
If a 'foist' and his glance of contempt is enough
Why he dives for his snuff-box and takes only snuff.
Here the man who is neighbour to famed Mr. Squib,
(He may call us *obscure*, and perhaps tell us we fib)
The 'spirited bidder' (for whom we sha'n't say)
Is beginning as usual his work of the day,
And before the great clock of the Abbey strikes four
Will have made some two hundred bold biddings or more,
Till Clarke, justly incensed with the fellow's assurance,
Lets him in with a look of affected endurance,
Saying, 'Sir, 'tis your own—give you joy of the lot, it
Has long been contested and now you have got it.'
Oh to see how he changes from yellow to blue,
As he answers, 'I'm ready to yield it to you;
I have *run* up the thing, but if called on to *pay*
Why I think I must finish by running away.'
But a smile from his Patron sets all matters right,
And he boldly bids on in his pocket's despite.

Here the famous Count *Buff*—with his eyeglass and seals,
His rings on his fingers and spurs on his heels,
His straw-coloured wig and magniloquent air,
And his hat cocked aside like a clown at a fair,

Strutting up to some daub, with his hand o'er his brow,
And wiping the canvas, cries 'RUBENS I vow,
His colouring—relief—light and shadow are there—
His expression—his grouping—his breadth to a hair.
Then that CUYP there beside it's as pearly and clear,
As the first break of day at the spring of the year;
Though it can't be compared with that dewy METZU
So melting and mellow, so tasteful and true:
They've a charm above all that must make them divine;'
(Speaking under his breath) '*entre nous*, Sir, they're mine.
Yes, you're doubtless surprised that a man of my air,
Should thus chaffer in pictures, but list while I swear,
'Twas my love for the Arts, and I'm master of some,
That first made me DEALER, and led me to roam.
As for money, my friend, I would have you to know,
I care nothing about a few thousands or so;
There's my own private income, a mere bagatelle—
Just five thousand a year, which you know's pretty well,—
A trifle admitted, but surely enough
To buy a few baubles, and pay for one's snuff;
Then my wife, besides beauty, of which we'll be mum,
Has, fore God I declare it, two-thirds of a PLUM;
To say naught of an Uncle who lives in the Indies,
(By the way, can you tell me, my friend, how the wind is?)
Who has promised, and sure he can do it with ease,
To send us ere long a few lachs of rupees.
Then my private collection is worth—so they say—
Just a cool hundred thousand (not much by the way),
And my house and its trappings (pray speak if I bore)
Has been valued by some at a good hundred more.
As you guess, in my own hackney coach I came down,
To see how matters go,—and look after my own;
And thanks to yon pliable knights of the quill
I shall do pretty well by the sale at Fonthill.'
Here the white-trousered Dandy and black-whiskered Swell,
The lean sprig of fashion, the beau and the belle—
The Lord and the Lady—but few of the latter,—
Have all journeyed post-haste, not to buy but to chatter,—
To lounge, look about them, and prate at their ease,
Of Mieris, Correggio, and Paul Veronese.

But vainly the vender directs his keen glance
To many a gay group as the biddings advance,
Inattentive are they to the beam of his eye,
And he turns to Clarke, Lawford, and Rodd with a sigh,—
Mid sunshine and storm, mid report good and ill,
The heroes and props of the sale at Fonthill.

Here Colnaghi, Thorpe, Phillips and Farquhar, good men,
We could sketch to the life with four strokes of our pen;
But we think we had better not touch off a verse on all
Lest some ill-natured booby should say we've grown personal.
However to prove that no evil we mean them,
We'll give them a sweet-tempered couplet between them,
The two first are good fellows we own with good will,
The two last are as good—at the sale at Fonthill.

There are auctions for ever unchangingly dull,
Like a long winter night ere the moon's at its full,
Selling on—selling on, but in bidders so slender,
That ere buyers are caught, half asleep is the vender;
Where excepting for brokers, booksellers, and one
Like the spirited Lawford, no sale could go on.
Where Report, like a spectre called up from the tomb,
Whispers 'Humbug' and 'Trick' and bids buyers be dumb.
These are not the auctions, 'tis nothing like these
That has taught Jemmy Christie all parties to please,
That has given him a power he can wield at his will,
With the flower of West-enders his saleroom to fill,
And sans sweeteners or spoonies, to kick up a pother
To get biddings in plenty of one sort or other.
'Tis plain honesty lifts him so far o'er his peers
And has crowned him the Emperor of Town Auctioneers;—
With that sprightliness ever in motion, which plays
On the eye and the pocket, and charms us both ways:
Now here and now there, wiling cash as it flies
From the eyes to the purse, from the purse to the eyes.
If in pictures he deals, such his elegant ease,
You would swear he was born to sell nothing but these;
And his passing mistakes do but serve to awaken
New mirth, while his credit stands firm and unshaken.

If in Books he dilates—he's as deftly at home,
Be they Novels from Paris or Classics from Rome;
If on Music—he knows the deep art to unriddle,
When from far-famed Cremona he sells you a fiddle;
In short such the power of his spells, I've been told,
He can turn what he touches, like Croesus, to gold;
And dull before him, you may say what you will,
Is the keen Auctioneer of the Sale at Fonthill.

A.A.W.

BECKFORD'S TOWER

(Lansdown, Bath)

Here on this lofty tower alone I stand
And gaze entranced upon this lovely land
Which poets, old and new, combine to praise,
Tho' its full beauty still eludes their lays.

Here BECKFORD came in his declining years,
And built this monument, which still uprears
Its towering height on Lansdown's placid scene;
A striking landmark midst the landscape green.

The only relic now of him who spent
His strength and substance seeking for content
Of mind and spirit—ranging far and wide,
To feed desires that would not be denied.

Save for the massive stone that marks his grave
By yonder moat, where grasses gently wave,
Nothing remains but this great tower, to tell
Of him who lived his life neath Fortune's spell.

Boyhood and youth from every care were free,
His varying moods were met indulgently:
Heir to great riches, nought could ever bind
To dull pursuits his bold, romantic mind.

Manhood to him still greater freedom brought,
The world of action, and the world of thought
Claimed his full days: incessantly he roved
Seeking the costly treasures that he loved.

The mystery and magic of the East
His mind provided with a constant feast:
'Vathek' his fitful genius did enhance,
(That weird, fantastic, swifly-writ Romance).

The slave of beauty, and of treasures rare,
His wealth a splendour bought beyond compare:
Caskets and carvings, chalices of gold,
And peerless pictures of a price untold.

A stately 'Abbey' by his order rose
There at Fonthill, bizarre and grandiose
And, though its towers, through faulty building fell,
Yet for a time it served his purpose well.

Reduced in fortune, here at last he came
To end his days, and set his seal to fame
Such as it was—ephemeral at its best,
And yielding nought that gave his spirit rest.

Yet at the last ambition did contrive
Some means to keep his memory alive:
This massive tower remains, that all may see
The final freak of ingrained vanity!

Silent it broods above the claustered dead,
Guarding the secrets that from earth hath fled:
Warning beholders that Life's little day
Twixt gleam and gloom will soon have passed away!

W. GREGORY HARRIS

THIS BOOK
IS PUBLISHED BY
THE AYLESFORD PRESS
158 MORETON ROAD, UPTON, WIRRAL, CHESHIRE.

IT IS PHOTOSET IN 11/12 TIMES ROMAN,
PRINTED BY
THE HILBRE PRESS, WIRRAL, CHESHIRE
ON AN ANTIQUE LAID PAPER
AND BOUND IN CLOTH BY
THOMAS LOUGHLIN, CANNING PLACE, LIVERPOOL

THE EDITION IS LIMITED TO
300 NUMBERED COPIES

192.